D1064871

EARTH
Our Home in the Solar System

by Ellen Lawrence

Consultants:

Suzy Gazlay, MA
Recipient, Presidential Award for Excellence in Science Teaching

Kevin Yates
Fellow of the Royal Astronomical Society

Published in 2014 by Ruby Tuesday Books Ltd.

Copyright © 2014 Ruby Tuesday Books Ltd.

Editor: Mark J. Sachner
Designer: Emma Randall

Photo Credits:
NASA: Cover, 4–5, 6, 8, 10, 12, 13 (bottom), 19
(bottom), 20–21; Ruby Tuesday Books: 7, 9, 22;
Shutterstock: 11, 13 (top), 14, 15 (top), 15 (bottom),
16–17, 18, 19 (top).

Library of Congress Control Number: 2013939984

ISBN 978-1-909673-06-9

Printed and published in the United States of America

For further information including rights and
permissions requests, please contact our Customer
Service Department at 877-337-8577.

Contents

Words shown in **bold** in the text are
explained in the glossary.

Our Amazing Home in Space

Imagine you are aboard a spacecraft waiting to blast off from Earth.

You hear the words "three, two, one, zero, and lift-off!"

Your spacecraft shakes as it is carried into the sky by a huge rocket.

Soon you are speeding through space at thousands of miles per hour.

You look out of the window and see a bright blue, green, and brown world.

It's **planet** Earth, our amazing home in space!

This photo of Earth was taken by a **satellite** in 2012. Just think. You were somewhere on this beautiful planet when the photo was taken!

The Solar System

Earth is moving through space at over 66,000 miles per hour (107,000 km/h).

It is moving in a huge circle around the Sun.

Earth is one of eight planets circling the Sun.

The planets are called Mercury, Venus, Earth, Mars, Jupiter, Saturn, Uranus, and Neptune.

Icy **comets** and large rocks, called **asteroids**, are also moving around the Sun.

Together, the Sun, the planets, and other space objects are called the **solar system**.

Most of the asteroids in the solar system are in a ring called the asteroid belt.

An asteroid

The Solar System
Earth is the third planet from the Sun.

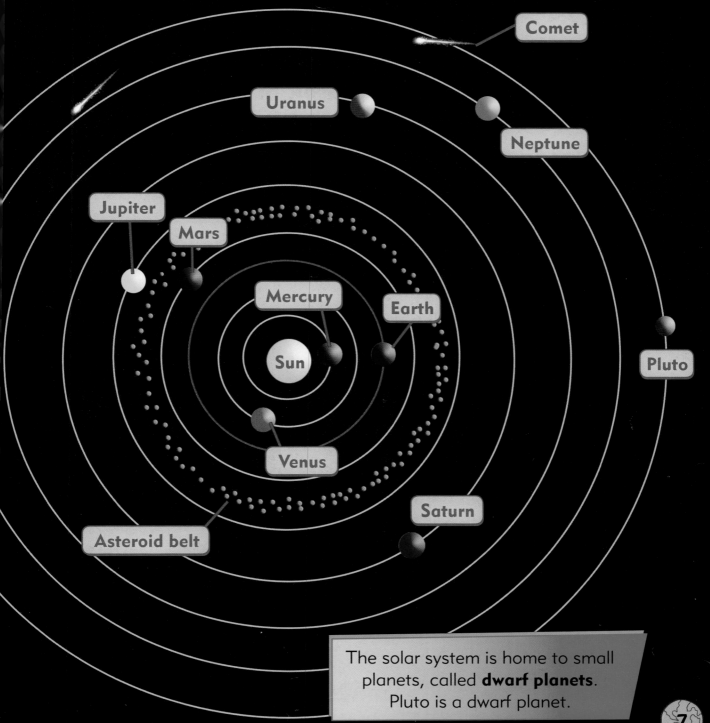

Comet

Uranus

Neptune

Jupiter

Mars

Mercury

Earth

Sun

Pluto

Venus

Saturn

Asteroid belt

The solar system is home to small planets, called **dwarf planets**. Pluto is a dwarf planet.

7

Earth's Amazing ☆☆ Journey

The time it takes a planet to **orbit**, or circle, the Sun once is called its year.

It takes Earth just over 365 days to orbit the Sun.

So a year on Earth lasts 365 days.

To orbit the Sun once, Earth must travel a long distance.

It makes a journey of about 584 million miles (940 million km).

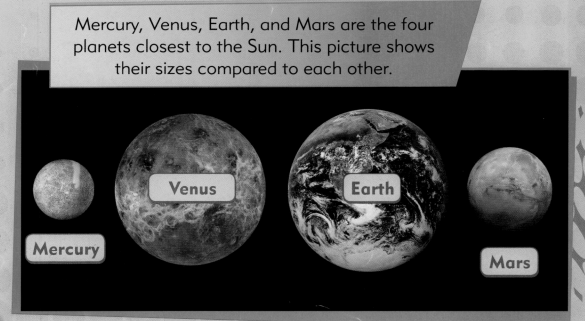

Mercury, Venus, Earth, and Mars are the four planets closest to the Sun. This picture shows their sizes compared to each other.

Mercury

Venus

Earth

Mars

Earth's Journey Around The Sun

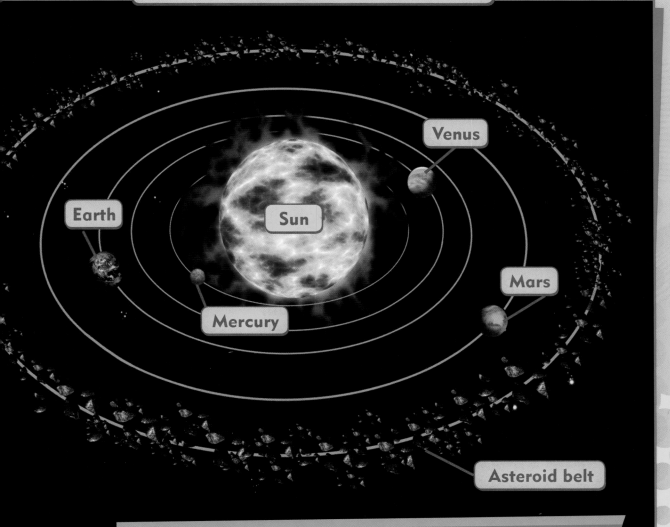

You might think you are sitting still reading this book. In fact, you and everything else on Earth are zooming at high speed around the Sun!

Spinning Through Space

As a planet orbits the Sun, it also spins, or **rotates**, like a top.

It takes Earth 24 hours to rotate once.

The reason we have day and night is because Earth is spinning.

When the place where you live faces toward the Sun, it is daytime for you.

As it spins away from the Sun's light, darkness falls and it is night.

Earth is slightly tilted to one side as it spins.

Earth

This picture shows how day and night look on Earth. It's daytime on the half of the planet that's facing the Sun. On the other half, it's nighttime.

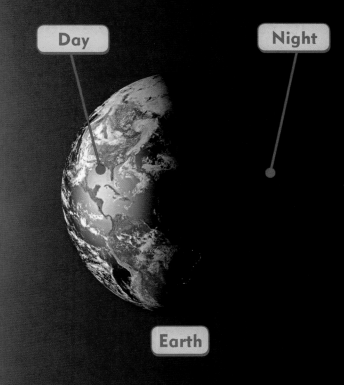

Day

Night

Sun

Earth

This picture shows Earth and the Sun very close together. In real life, Earth is about 93 million miles (150 million km) from the Sun.

Earth's Space Neighbor

Planet Earth travels through space with its closest neighbor, the Moon.

The Moon is orbiting Earth.

It takes the Moon just over 27 days to orbit Earth once.

When we see the Moon in the sky, it looks white or grayish-white.

That's because the Sun's light is shining on the Moon and lighting it up.

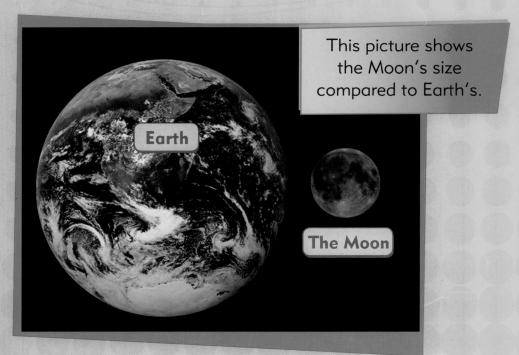

Earth

The Moon

This picture shows the Moon's size compared to Earth's.

The Moon looks as if it changes shape, but it doesn't really. As the Moon travels around Earth, we see different parts of its shining surface.

These photos show some of the different ways that we see the Moon from Earth.

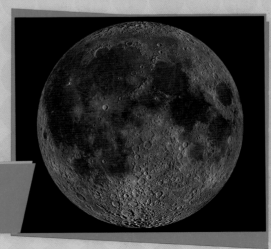

This is a close-up photo of the Moon's surface.

A Closer Look at Earth

If you could cut Earth in half, you'd see that it is made up of different layers.

The outer layer of Earth is a thin, rocky crust.

Beneath the crust is a layer of super-hot rock that flows and oozes like soft taffy.

Deeper down is a layer of metal that is so hot, it's melted and turned to liquid.

In the center of the planet is a solid metal ball.

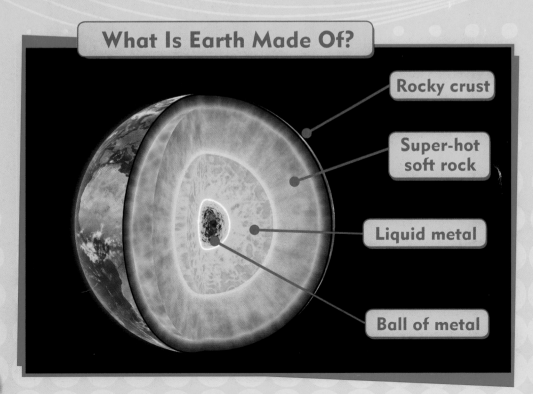

What Is Earth Made Of?

Rocky crust

Super-hot soft rock

Liquid metal

Ball of metal

All around Earth, there is a thick layer of **gases** called an **atmosphere**. This picture shows how the atmosphere looks from space.

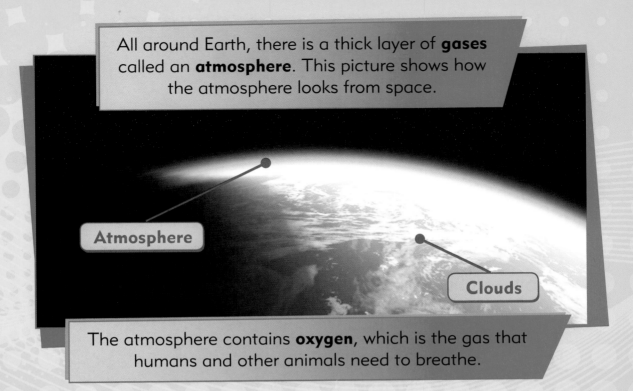

Atmosphere

Clouds

The atmosphere contains **oxygen**, which is the gas that humans and other animals need to breathe.

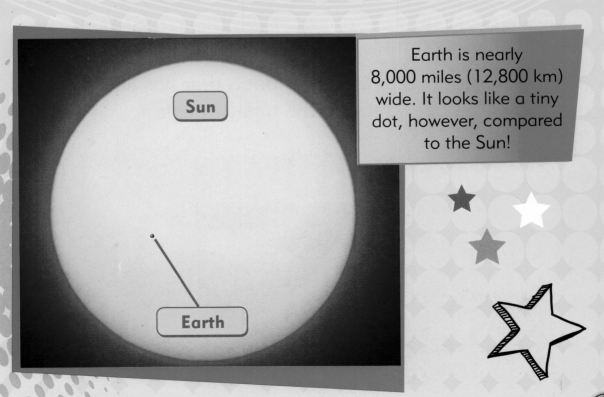

Sun

Earth

Earth is nearly 8,000 miles (12,800 km) wide. It looks like a tiny dot, however, compared to the Sun!

The Blue Planet

Earth has been nicknamed "The Blue Planet," because it looks blue from space.

That's because about three-quarters of its surface is covered by water.

There is liquid water in oceans, lakes, and rivers.

There is also frozen water in icy, super-cold places such as the North and South Poles.

Scientists have discovered ice and water on other planets and moons in the solar system.

Earth is the only planet or moon that has liquid water on its surface all the time, though.

A lake

Earth's oceans are thousands of miles wide. In places, they are over 4 miles (6.4 km) deep.

The Blue Planet

This photo shows the ice-covered ground at the South Pole. In places, the ice is 3 miles (4.8 km) thick.

A Very Special Planet

Earth is a very special planet in one important way.

It is the only planet in the solar system where we know there is life.

Scientists think there are over 8 million different types of living things on Earth.

Our planet is home to plants, animals, and tiny living things such as **microbes**.

It is also home to one super-intelligent type of animal. That's you!

Microbe

This is a close-up photo of a microbe. Microbes are so small, we can't see them with our eyes.

There are hundreds of thousands of different types of plants and animals on Earth.

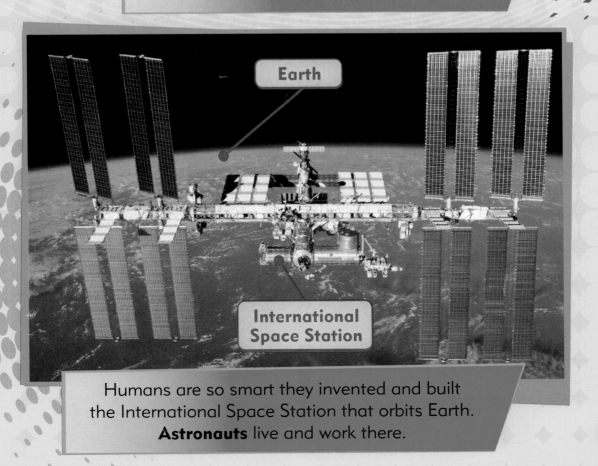

Earth

International Space Station

Humans are so smart they invented and built the International Space Station that orbits Earth. **Astronauts** live and work there.

Earth Fact File

Here are some key facts about Earth, the third planet from the Sun.

How Earth got its name

The word "Earth" is a very old word for "ground."

Planet sizes

This picture shows the sizes of the solar system's planets compared to each other.

Sun

Mercury Earth

Venus Mars

Jupiter

Saturn

Uranus

Neptune

Earth's size

About 7,918 miles (12,742 km) across

How long it takes for Earth to rotate once

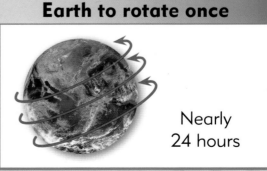

Nearly 24 hours

Earth's distance from the Sun

The closest Earth gets to the Sun is 91,402,640 miles (147,098,291 km).

The farthest Earth gets from the Sun is 94,509,460 miles (152,098,233 km).

Length of Earth's orbit around the Sun

584,019,311 miles (939,887,974 km)

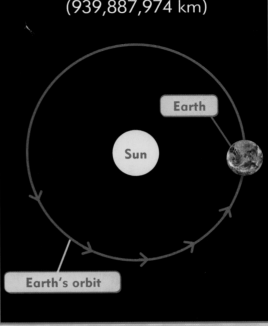

Earth

Sun

Earth's orbit

Average speed at which Earth orbits the Sun

66,622 miles per hour (107,218 km/h)

Length of a year on Earth

Just over 365 days

Earth's Moons

Earth has one moon.

Temperature on Earth

Highest: 136°F (58°C)
Lowest: -126°F (-88°C)

Get Crafty

☆ ☆ Solar System Concentration game

Sun

Sun

1. Cut a large piece of construction paper into 30 rectangular cards.

2. Choose 15 space objects and draw or paint a pair of cards for each object. You can include the Sun, the Moon, the eight planets, asteroids, and comets.

3. Write the names of the objects onto the cards, too.

4. Now shuffle the cards and lay them face down, and you're ready to play solar system concentration.

Sun	Earth	Moon	Moon	Mercury

Venus	Mars	Jupiter	Saturn	Uranus

Neptune	Asteroid	Asteroid	Comet	Rocket
				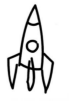

asteroid (AS-teh-royd) A large rock that is orbiting the Sun. An asteroid can be as small as a car or bigger than a mountain.

astronaut (AS-troh-nawt) A person who is trained to go into space in a spacecraft.

atmosphere (AT-muh-sfeer) A layer of gases around a planet, moon, or star.

comet (KAH-mit) A space object made of ice, rock, and dust that is orbiting the Sun.

dwarf planet (DWARF PLAN-et) A round object in space that is orbiting the Sun. Dwarf planets are much smaller than the eight main planets.

gas (GASS) A substance, such as oxygen or helium, that does not have a definite shape or size.

microbe (MY-krobe) A living thing that is so tiny it can't be seen with your eyes. The germs that make people sick are types of microbes.

orbit (OR-bit) To circle, or move around, another object.

oxygen (OX-ih-jin) An invisible gas in the air that you and other living things need to breathe.

planet (PLAN-et) A large object in space that is orbiting the Sun. Some planets, such as Earth, are made of rock. Others, such as Jupiter, are made of gases and liquids.

rotate (ROH-tate) To spin around.

satellite (SAT-uh-lite) An object that orbits a planet. Satellites are used for beaming TV and cell phone signals around Earth.

solar system (SOH-ler SIS-tem) The Sun and all the objects that orbit it, such as planets, their moons, asteroids, and comets.

Index

Read More

Hughes, Catherine D.
*First Big Book of Space
(National Geographic Little
Kids)*. Washington, D.C.:
The National Geographic
Society (2012).

Oxlade, Chris.
*Space Watch: The Earth
(Eye on Space)*. New York:
PowerKids Press (2011).

Learn More Online

To learn more about Earth, go to
www.rubytuesdaybooks.com/earth